Y0-DDP-206

NEW WEIGHT WATCHERS FREESTYLE COOKBOOK 2020

BY CRISTINA JACOBS

© Copyright 2019 - All rights reserved.

All rights reserved. No part of this publication may be reproduced, distributed, or transmitted in any form or by any means, including photocopying, recording, or other electronic or mechanical methods, without the prior written permission of the publisher.

CONTENTS

EVERYTHING YOU NEED TO KNOW ABOUT FREESTYLE POINTS

Freestyle points are one great innovation that has made it easy for people to understand the Weight Watchers program and integrate into their lifestyle. With Freestyle points, you do not have to change your old dietary habits. That is why it has achieved tremendous success since its inception.

Freestyle points as mentioned before ranges from 1 to 10. You do not feel like you are on a diet when following Freestyle 2018 diet. Each recipe covered in the book carries its Freestyle point values. Earlier, Weight Watchers program allowed consuming 30 Freestyle points per day, which has been reduced to 23 in its latest 2018 version. Now it makes it clear to understand how these points work. For example, you can choose any breakfast, lunch, dinner, dessert, snack, etc. to consume in a day and all you need to do is keep the total Freestyle point values to equal to or less than 23 points. Yes, this is as simple as that.

WEIGHT WATCHERS DIET: FOODS TO EAT

As the program focuses on allowing people to eat meals they like, all foods can be consumed, but the focus primarily is on consuming them in moderation. As the diet aims to improve holistic health, the focus is on eating health transforming foods including healthy vegetables, lean meat cuts, nuts, fresh greens, oils with healthy fats, and fresh fruits. When it comes to carbohydrates and cooking oils, healthier versions are preferable such as brown rice, beans, oatmeal, whole grains, olive oil, etc.

BENEFITS OF FOLLOWING THE FREESTYLE DIET

Weight Watchers program is focused on naturally delivering effective weight loss without putting your body through strenuous exercise regime or food restricting diet schedule. The key benefit of the diet is obvious; however, the diet offers many lifestyle benefits to improve your way of living significantly.

Less dietary restrictions
Absolute no food restriction is a great positive aspect where you are the boss of your meal plan. You can make your meal plans based on its allotted SmartPoints for each

recipe. It does not mean that you can stuff yourself with doughnuts, burgers, fries and soft drinks. Of course, the diet has restrictions, but it does not put you through a complicated meal schedule.

Sustainable long term results

Weight Watchers program helps you to achieve weight loss that you can maintain for years and decades. It adapts you to a new smart way of living life, which is like adapting to a new healthy habit. People have reported losing 1-2 pounds in just one week of following Weight Watchers programme under the guidance of their trained experts. The weight loss results are steady and consistent.

Healthy homely food

As you are preparing meals by yourself at home using Instant Pot, one significant advantage is of consuming healthy meals at home instead of relying on commercial restaurant made foods.

The diet has introduced more than 200 foods in its zero Freestyle point category. These foods can be consumed without worrying about its nutritional composition. Popular foods with zero points are.

- Beans
- Grapes
- Garlic
- Fresh veggies (limited consumption of avocado, potatoes, olives, and sweet potatoes)
- Lentils
- Lemons
- Most green veggies such as spinach, lettuce, etc.
- Berries
- All bean types
- Turkey breasts
- Chicken breasts
- Egg whites
- All fish types
- Non-fat yogurts
- Fresh fruits or canned fruits (without added sugar)
- Mushrooms
- Tofu
- Okra
- Broccoli
- Bananas
- Asparagus

When you aim to lose weight, it is not a onetime thing as you need to maintain the results for the long term. Keep in mind following simple tips to get the best out of Freestyle diet.

Hydration – Keep your body ideally hydrated to boost metabolism and helps in sustainably achieving weight loss. Drink 14-16 ounces of water 30-45 minutes before taking your meals. It helps in keeping your appetite under control.

Sugar Control – If you have a habit of adding sugar to foods and drinks, you should start staying away from it. Try to replace sugar with naturally sweet fruits or sugar substitutes like stevia, maple syrup, etc. Buy groceries that are without any added sugar.

Morning Coffee – Having a cup of hot steaming coffee in the morning is an excellent enabler for metabolism boost and also provides anti-oxidants to your body. Unsweetened coffee is preferable.

WEIGHT WATCHERS DIET: RESTRICTED FOODS

Foods that off-limit are very obvious ones that are loaded with high saturated fats, complex carbohydrates and empty calories including cakes, cookies, crackers, fried foods, commercial fast foods, commercial pizzas and burgers, candies, processed meats and sugar-based soft drinks, fruits, and other beverages.

Bacon Egg Muffins

Prep Time: 8-10 min.

Cooking Time: 25-30 min.

Number of Servings: 3

Freestyle Points per Serving: 4

Ingredients:

- ¼ cup skim milk
- 6 egg whites
- 6 eggs
- ½ cup shredded part-skim mozzarella
- Pepper and salt as per taste
- 1 zucchini, cut to dice
- 6 pieces turkey bacon, chop into small pieces

Directions:

1. Preheat an oven to 375°F.
2. Spray 6 muffins with cooking spray.
3. Take a skillet or saucepan (medium size preferable); heat it over a medium cooking flame.
4. Add some cooking spray and heat it.
5. Add the bacon and cook until crisp for 5-6 minutes. Add the bacon to a plate and discard bacon fat.
6. Add the zucchini to the saucepan and sauté until tender for 4-5 minutes. Add with the bacon.
7. Take a mixing bowl (either medium or large size), crack and whisk the eggs. Season as needed.
8. Mix in the milk, cheese, zucchini, and bacon.
9. Add muffin tins; bake for 20 minutes. Serve warm.

Nutritional Values (Per Serving):

Calories – 246

Fat – 14g

Saturated Fats – 6g

Trans Fats - 0g

Carbohydrates – 6g

Fiber – 1g

Sodium – 754mg

Protein – 27g

Broccoli Egg Muffins

Prep Time: 8-10 min.

Cooking Time: 13-15 min.

Number of Servings: 6

Freestyle Points per Serving: 4

Ingredients:

- 2 cups broccoli, steamed and chopped into small pieces
- Pepper and salt as per taste
- ½ tablespoon Dijon mustard
- 2 green onions, chop into small pieces
- ¾ cup shredded cheddar cheese, reduced fat
- 4 egg whites
- 8 eggs

Directions:

1. Preheat an oven to 350°F.
2. Spray 12 muffins with cooking spray.
3. Take a mixing bowl (either medium or large size), crack and whisk the eggs. Mix in the pepper, salt, mustard, and egg whites.
4. Mix in the cheese, green onions, and broccoli.
5. Add the mix into muffin tins. Bake for 12 minutes or until puffs up.
6. Serve warm.

Nutritional Values (Per Serving):

Calories – 184

Fat – 9g

Saturated Fats – 4g

Trans Fats - 0g

Carbohydrates – 4g

Fiber – 1g

Sodium – 312mg

Protein – 16g

Peanut Butter Oats

Prep Time: 8-10 min.

Cooking Time: 0 min.

Number of Servings: 1

Freestyle Points per Serving: 7

Ingredients:

- ¾ cup almond milk
- 1 tablespoon jam, sugar-free
- 1 tablespoon peanut butter
- ½ cup old-fashioned oats

Directions:

1. Take a mixing bowl (either medium or large size), add and mix in the ingredients except the jam in the bowl to mix well with each other.
2. Cover the bowl and set in the fridge overnight.
3. Take out in the morning and add a jam on top. Serve.

Nutritional Values (Per Serving):

Calories – 226

Fat – 8g

Saturated Fats – 1g

Trans Fats - 0g

Carbohydrates – 32g

Fiber – 7g

Sodium – 97mg

Protein – 9g

Apple Honey Oats

Prep Time: 8-10 min.

Cooking Time: 10-15 min.

Number of Servings: 4

Freestyle Points per Serving: 4

Ingredients:

- 1 teaspoon vanilla extract
- 1 gala apple, peeled and cut to dice
- 2 tablespoons honey
- 1 cup milk
- 1/8 tsp salt
- 1 teaspoon cinnamon
- 2 cups water
- ½ cup steel cut oats

Directions:

1. Take a skillet or saucepan (medium size preferable); heat it over a medium cooking flame.
2. Add the vanilla, honey, milk, and water and boil the mix.
3. Add the oatmeal and apples and mix well.
4. Turn down the cooking flame to low setting; cover the saucepan or skillet and let the mix simmer for about 8-10 minutes (stir in between).
5. Stir in the salt and cinnamon; cook for 1-2 minutes. Serve warm.

Nutritional Values (Per Serving):

Calories - 161

Fat – 2g

Saturated Fats – 1g

Trans Fats - 0g

Carbohydrates – 26g

Fiber – 7g

Sodium – 43mg

Protein – 5g

Berry Banana Pancakes

Prep Time: 8-10 min.

Cooking Time: 5 min.

Number of Servings: 2

Freestyle Points per Serving: 1

Ingredients:

- 1 teaspoon baking powder
- 1 banana, mashed well
- ¼ teaspoon cinnamon
- 1 teaspoon vanilla
- 2 egg whites

Directions:

1. Take a skillet or saucepan (medium size preferable); heat it over medium cooking flame.
2. Take a mixing bowl (either medium or large size), crack and whisk the egg whites.
3. Stir in the cinnamon, vanilla, and baking powder.
4. Add the banana and mix; divide batter into 4 parts.
5. Add the batter, spread to make round and cook for 2 minutes, flip and cook for 30-45 seconds more.
6. Repeat process for remaining batter. Serve with fresh berries.

Nutritional Values (Per Serving):

Calories – 237

Fat – 1g

Saturated Fats – 0g

Trans Fats - 0g

Carbohydrates – 23g

Fiber – 6g

Sodium – 396mg

Protein – 9g

Breakfast Casserole

Prep Time: 8-10 min.

Cooking Time: 45 min.

Number of Servings: 4

Freestyle Points per Serving: 4

Ingredients:

- 4 eggs
- 2 teaspoons cinnamon
- 1 cup milk
- 1 1/3 cup egg whites
- 2 apples, peeled and cut to dice
- 8 slices bread, low calorie

Directions:

1. Lightly grease a casserole dish (9x13-inch) with cooking spray. Preheat an oven to 350°F.
2. In a microwave-safe mixing bowl, mix 1 teaspoon cinnamon and apples.
3. Microwave the mix for 2-3 minutes.
4. In the dish, add the bread slices and cooked apples.
5. In a mixing bowl, whisk fresh milk, egg whites, and eggs.
6. Add the mix over the dish; bake for 45 minutes.
7. Serve warm.

Nutritional Values (Per Serving):

Calories – 376

Fat – 9g

Saturated Fats – 3g

Trans Fats - 0g

Carbohydrates – 36g

Fiber – 12g

Sodium – 752mg

Protein – 24g

Cheese Basil Frittata

Prep Time: 8-10 min.

Cooking Time: 20 min.

Number of Servings: 4

Freestyle Points per Serving: 7

Ingredients:

- 1 tablespoon fresh parsley, chopped into small pieces
- 2 tablespoons basil, chopped into small pieces
- ½ cup crumbled goat cheese
- 1 cup cherry tomatoes, halved
- 2 tablespoons chives, chopped into small pieces
- ¼ cup milk
- 8 large eggs
- ¼ teaspoon ground pepper
- ½ teaspoon salt

Directions:

1. Preheat an oven to 450°F. Lightly grease a casserole dish (9x13-inch) with cooking spray.
2. Take a mixing bowl (either medium or large size), add in the pepper, salt, milk, and eggs in the bowl to mix well with each other.
3. In the dish, add the herbs and tomatoes. Top with the cheese and add the egg mixture over it.
4. Bake for 20 minutes or until tops are set.
5. Serve warm.

Nutritional Values (Per Serving):

Calories – 234

Fat – 14g

Saturated Fats – 5g

Trans Fats - 0g

Carbohydrates – 9g

Fiber – 4g

Sodium – 448mg

Protein – 19g

Tomato Salmon Morning

Prep Time: 8-10 min.

Cooking Time: 15 min.

Number of Servings: 2

Freestyle Points per Serving: 0

Ingredients:

- 1 clove of garlic, minced
- Small jalapeno pepper, chopped into small pieces
- 1 plum tomato, chopped into small pieces
- ½ small onion, chopped into small pieces
- 1 teaspoon apple cider vinegar
- ¼ teaspoon salt
- 3 dashes of any hot sauce
- ½ teaspoon chili powder
- ¼ teaspoon ground cumin
- 2 (4-ounce each) salmon fillets

Directions:

1. Preheat an oven to 400°F.
2. In a food processor or blender, mix the all the Ingredients except for the fillets.
3. Place the salmon in a roasting skillet or saucepan; add the blender mix on top.
4. Roast in the oven for 15 minutes or until the salmon gets flaky.
5. Serve warm.

Nutritional Values (Per Serving):

Calories - 208

Fat – 11g

Saturated Fats – 2g

Trans Fats - 0g

Carbohydrates – 3g

Fiber – 1g

Sodium – 86mg

Protein – 23g

Ham Egg Frittata

Prep Time: 8-10 min.

Cooking Time: 10 min.

Number of Servings: 4-6

Freestyle Points per Serving: 2

Ingredients:

- 8 ounces ham, chopped
- 1 teaspoon white pepper
- 1 tablespoon lemon zest
- 1 teaspoon olive oil
- 1 teaspoon salt
- ½ teaspoon paprika
- ½ cup parsley, chopped
- 7 eggs
- ½ cup milk
- 1 tomato, chopped

Directions:

1. Beat the eggs in the mixing bowl. Mix in the milk, salt, paprika, white pepper, and lemon zest.
2. Blend the mix in a blender. Mix in the ham and tomatoes.
3. Take an Instant Pot; open the top lid.
4. Coat the pot using cooking oil. Add the ham mix in the cooking pot. Top with the parsley.
5. Close the top lid and make sure the valve is sealed.
6. Press "STEAM" cooking function. Adjust cooking time to 10 minutes.
7. Allow pressure to build and cook the ingredients for the set time.
8. After the set cooking time ends, press "CANCEL" and then press "QPR". Instant Pot will quickly release pressure.
9. Open the top lid, add the cooked mixture in serving plates.
10. Serve warm.

Nutritional Values (Per Serving):

Calories - 215

Fat – 13g

Carbohydrates – 6.5g

Fiber – 1g

Sodium - 346mg

Protein – 17.5g

Spinach Omelet Morning

Prep Time: 8-10 min.

Cooking Time: 6 min.

Number of Servings: 4-5

Freestyle Points per Serving: 2

Ingredients:

- ½ cup milk
- 1 teaspoon salt
- 1 tablespoon olive oil
- 2 cups spinach, chopped
- 8 eggs
- 1 teaspoon ground black pepper
- 4 ounces Parmesan cheese

Directions:

1. Add the eggs to a mixing bowl and whisk them. Mix in the spinach.
2. Mix in the milk, salt, olive oil, and black pepper. Stir the mixture well.
3. Take an Instant Pot; open the top lid.
4. Coat the pot using cooking oil. Add the mix in the cooking pot.
5. Close the top lid and make sure the valve is sealed.
6. Press "STEAM" cooking function. Adjust cooking time to 6 minutes.
7. Allow pressure to build and cook the ingredients for the set time.
8. After the set cooking time ends, press "CANCEL" and then press "QPR". Instant Pot will quickly release pressure.
9. Open the top lid, add the cooked mixture in serving plates.
10. Serve warm; top with the cheese.

Nutritional Values (Per Serving):

Calories - 327

Fat – 18.5g

Carbohydrates – 12.5g

Fiber – 0g

Sodium - 324mg

Protein – 25g

Spiced Ham Eggs

Prep Time: 8-10 min.

Cooking Time: 4 min.

Number of Servings: 3

Freestyle Points per Serving: 3

Ingredients:

- 1 teaspoon salt
- 3 eggs, beaten
- 6 ounces ham, cooked
- ½ teaspoon ground white pepper
- 1 teaspoon paprika
- ¼ teaspoon ground ginger
- 2 tablespoons chives

Directions:

1. Take three small ramekins; coat them with oil spray.
2. Add the eggs to the ramekins.
3. Sprinkle the salt, black pepper, and paprika.
4. Close the top lid and make sure the valve is sealed.
5. Press "STEAM" cooking function. Adjust cooking time to 4 minutes.
6. Allow pressure to build and cook the ingredients for the set time.
7. After the set cooking time ends, press "CANCEL" and then press "QPR". Instant Pot will quickly release pressure.
8. Open the top lid, add the ramekins in serving plates.
9. Chop the ham and chives; combine them.
10. Mix in the ground ginger.
11. Serve the ramekins with the ham mix on top.

Nutritional Values (Per Serving):

Calories – 213

Fat – 11g

Carbohydrates – 7.5g

Fiber – 2g

Sodium - 234mg

Protein – 18.5g

Steak Bean Soup

Prep Time: 8-10 min.

Cooking Time: 25-30 min.

Number of Servings: 8

Freestyle Points per Serving: 1

Ingredients:

- ½ cup chop into small pieces, onions
- 1 teaspoon Italian seasoning mix
- ½ teaspoon olive oil
- ½ pound lean round steak, sliced
- ¼ teaspoon garlic salt
- ¼ teaspoon pepper
- 1 can tomatoes, diced
- ½ cup chop into small pieces, carrots
- 2 ½ cups shredded cabbage
- ¼ cup snipped parsley
- 1 can white kidney beans, rinsed and drained
- 2 cans beef broth, fat-free and low-sodium

Directions:

1. Take a skillet or saucepan (medium size preferable); heat it over a medium cooking flame.
2. Add the oil and heat it.
3. Stir in the meat and onions. Stir-cook for 3 minutes.
4. Mix in the seasoning mix, garlic, salt, and pepper; cook for 2 minutes.
5. Mix and stir the tomatoes, carrots, kidney beans and broth.
6. Boil and allow to simmer for 20 minutes.
7. Add the cabbages and parsley; simmer for 5 more minutes.
8. Serve warm.

Nutritional Values (Per Serving):

Calories – 137

Fat – 2g

Saturated Fats – 1g

Trans Fats - 0g

Carbohydrates – 15g

Fiber – 4g

Sodium – 654mg

Protein – 12g

Chicken Corn Spinach Soup

Prep Time: 8-10 min.

Cooking Time: 70-80 min.

Number of Servings: 8

Freestyle Points per Serving: 3

Ingredients:

- 4 cups baby spinach
- 1 white onion, cut to dice
- 3 cloves minced roasted garlic
- 1 pound boneless skinless chicken breasts, roasted and shredded
- 2 cups frozen corn, thawed
- 1 yellow bell pepper, cut to dice
- 3 cups chicken broth, low-sodium
- 1 tablespoon cumin
- 1 tablespoon salt
- 3 poblano peppers, roasted and cut to dice
- 5 cups water
- 1 teaspoon black pepper
- 1 cup fat-free sour cream

Directions:

1. Take a cooking pot or deep saucepan (medium size preferable); heat it over a medium cooking flame.
2. Combine all Ingredients, except for the sour cream in the pot. Mix until well-combined.
3. Boil the mix; let the mix simmer for about 60 minutes (stir in between).
4. Mix in the cream and continue cooking for 10 minutes.
5. Serve warm.

Nutritional Values (Per Serving):

Calories - 141

Fat – 3g

Saturated Fats – 0g

Trans Fats - 0g

Carbohydrates – 14g

Fiber – 2g

Sodium – 194mg

Protein – 15g

Tomato Herb Soup

Prep Time: 8-10 min.

Cooking Time: 15 min.

Number of Servings: 4

Freestyle Points per Serving: 5

Ingredients:

- ½ cup chop into small pieces, onions
- 1 stalk celery, chop into small pieces
- 3 tablespoons olive oil
- 2 cloves of garlic, minced
- 1 cup chicken broth, fat-free and low-sodium
- 1 cup skim milk
- 5 fresh basil leaves
- 1 14-ounce can tomato puree
- Pepper and salt as per taste
- 1 tablespoon cornstarch + 2 tablespoons water

Directions:

1. Mix the cornstarch with water in a bowl.
2. Add the onions and celery in a food processor and pulse until smooth.
3. Take a skillet or saucepan (medium size preferable); heat it over a medium cooking flame.
4. Add the oil and heat it.
5. Add the onion puree. Stir-cook for 3 minutes until translucent.
6. Add the garlic, broth, and tomato puree.
7. Season as per taste. Boil and simmer for 5 minutes.
8. Whisk in the milk, basil leaves, and cornstarch slurry; simmer for another 5 minutes.
9. Serve warm.

Nutritional Values (Per Serving):

Calories – 164

Fat – 10g

Saturated Fats – 1g

Trans Fats - 0g

Carbohydrates – 13g

Fiber – 2g

Sodium – 62mg

Protein – 5g

Potato Bean Stew

Prep Time: 8-10 min.

Cooking Time: NA

Number of Servings: 6

Freestyle Points per Serving: 4

Ingredients:

- 1 can red beans, drained and rinsed
- 4 cups vegetable broth
- 1 ¼ pounds sweet potatoes, peeled and cubed
- 2 cups cut to dice, tomatoes
- ½ cup water
- 1 onion, chopped into small pieces
- 1 teaspoon grated fresh ginger
- ½ teaspoon salt
- 1 bell pepper, chopped into small pieces
- 2 cloves of garlic, minced
- 1 teaspoon cumin powder
- ¼ teaspoon black pepper
- 3 tablespoons peanut butter

Directions:

1. Take a skillet or saucepan (medium size preferable); heat it over a medium cooking flame.
2. Add the broth and heat it. One by one add the ingredients except the peanut butter and mix well.
3. Cover the pan and simmer the mix until the veggies and bean turn soft.
4. Mix in the peanut butter and serve warm.

Nutritional Values (Per Serving):

Calories – 272

Fat – 7g

Saturated Fats – 1g

Trans Fats - 0g

Carbohydrates – 41g

Fiber – 8g

Sodium – 386mg

Protein – 9g

Chicken Mushroom Soup

Prep Time: 8-10 min.

Cooking Time: 20 min.

Number of Servings: 5

Freestyle Points per Serving: 5

Ingredients:

- 2 tablespoons lemon juice
- 1 teaspoon garlic, minced
- 1-pound boneless, skinless chicken breast
- 8-ounces fresh mushrooms, make slices
- 1 teaspoon fresh ginger, grated
- 3 scallions, thinly make slices
- 1 leek, green part only
- 2 cups fat-free chicken broth
- 2 tablespoons soy sauce, reduced sodium

Directions:

1. Take a cooking pot or deep saucepan (medium size preferable); heat it over a medium cooking flame.
2. Add all the ingredients except for the scallions and leeks.
3. Boil the mix; let the mix simmer for about 15 minutes.
4. Add the scallions and leeks; continue cooking for another 5 minutes. Serve warm.

Nutritional Values (Per Serving):

Calories – 72

Fat – 1g

Saturated Fats – 0g

Trans Fats - 0g

Carbohydrates – 3g

Fiber – 0g

Sodium – 423mg

Protein – 11g

Turkey Green Bean Soup

Prep Time: 8-10 min.

Cooking Time: 25 min.

Number of Servings: 6

Freestyle Points per Serving: 0

Ingredients:

- 1 ½ teaspoon minced garlic
- 1 ½ pound ground turkey breasts, skinless
- 1 cup chopped celery
- ½ cup onion, chopped
- 6 cups chicken broth, fat-free and low-sodium
- ½ cup frozen whole kernel corn
- 1 ½ teaspoon ground cumin
- 1 teaspoon chili powder
- 1 cup carrot, make slices
- ½ cup fresh green beans, make small pieces
- 2 bay leaves
- Cooking oil as needed
- 1 can tomatoes and green chilies, diced and undrained
- 6 tablespoons Monterey Jack cheese, grated
- 1 can kidney beans, rinsed and drained

Directions:

1. Take a skillet or saucepan (medium size preferable); heat it over a medium cooking flame.
2. Add the oil and heat it.
3. Add the celery, onion, garlic, and turkey. Stir and cook for 3 minutes.
4. Add the rest of the ingredient except the cheese.
5. Cover it; boil the mix. Let the mix simmer for about 18-20 minutes.
6. Serve warm with cheese on top.

Nutritional Values (Per Serving):

Calories – 204

Fat – 3g

Saturated Fats – 1g

Trans Fats - 0g

Carbohydrates – 21g

Fiber – 6g

Sodium – 532mg

Protein – 17g

Ginger Carrot Soup

Prep Time: 8-10 min.

Cooking Time: 35-40 min.

Number of Servings: 4

Freestyle Points per Serving: 3

Ingredients:

- 1 tablespoon fresh ginger, grated
- 1/4 cup sour cream, low-fat
- kosher salt and white pepper as per taste
- 2 tablespoon chives
- 1 tablespoon unsalted butter
- 1 large white onion, chopped
- 3 cups reduced-sodium vegetable broth
- 1 pound chopped, peeled carrots

Directions:

1. Take a skillet or saucepan (medium size preferable); heat it over a medium cooking flame.
2. Add the oil and heat it.
3. Add the onions and cook until turn soft for 5-6 minutes.
4. Add the broth, carrots, and ginger.
5. Cover it; boil the mix. Let the mixture simmer until the carrots become soft for 25-30 minutes.
6. Cool down the mix and make a puree in the blender.
7. Add back to the pan, mix the cream and heat the mix again.
8. Serve warm.

Nutritional Values (Per Serving):

Calories - 121

Fat – 6g

Saturated Fats – 4g

Trans Fats - 0g

Carbohydrates – 13g

Fiber – 3g

Sodium – 523mg

Protein – 2g

Chicken Brussels Soup

Prep Time: 8-10 min.

Cooking Time: 15 min.

Number of Servings: 4-5

Freestyle Points per Serving: 1

Ingredients:

- 1 cup water
- ½ teaspoon dried thyme
- 1 chopped medium leek, white part only
- 2 cans chicken broth, low sodium
- 8 ounces white mushrooms, make slices
- Pepper and salt as per taste
- 1-pound skinless chicken breasts make ½" inch pieces
- 8 ounces Brussels sprouts, halved

Directions:

1. Take a cooking pot or deep saucepan (medium size preferable); heat it over a medium cooking flame.
2. Add the ingredients and mix well.
3. Close the lid and bring to a boil; simmer for 15 minutes.
4. Serve warm.

Nutritional Values (Per Serving):

Calories – 174

Fat – 3g

Saturated Fats – 1g

Trans Fats - 0g

Carbohydrates – 8g

Fiber – 2g

Sodium – 168mg

Protein – 24g

Potato Chicken Roast

Prep Time: 8-10 min.

Cooking Time: 20 min.

Number of Servings: 5-6

Freestyle Points per Serving: 5

Ingredients:

- 2 cloves garlic, minced
- 2 teaspoons fresh thyme
- 1 teaspoon black pepper
- 1 large roasting chicken
- 2 teaspoons extra-virgin olive oil
- 1 teaspoon paprika
- 1 cup baby carrots
- 1 ½ cup water
- 1 teaspoon sea salt
- 2 stalks celery, chopped
- 2 medium potatoes, cubed

Directions:

1. Coat the chicken with the olive oil, garlic, thyme, black pepper, paprika, and salt. Add the celery and carrots inside the chicken cavity.
2. Take an Instant Pot; open the top lid.
3. Add the chicken and water in the cooking pot. Add the potatoes.
4. Close the top lid and make sure the valve is sealed.
5. Press "MANUAL" cooking function. Adjust cooking time to 20 minutes.
6. Allow pressure to build and cook the ingredients for the set time.
7. After the set cooking time ends, press "CANCEL" and then press "NPR". Instant Pot will slowly and naturally release the pressure for 8-10 minutes.
8. Open the top lid, add the cooked mixture in serving plates. Cook on sauté for a few minutes, if you want to thicken the sauce.
9. Serve warm.

Nutritional Values (Per Serving):

Calories – 276

Fat – 2.5g

Carbohydrates – 12g

Fiber – 1g

Sodium - 358mg

Protein – 23.5g

Coconut Curry Chicken

Prep Time: 8-10 min.

Cooking Time: 10 min.

Number of Servings: 5-6

Freestyle Points per Serving: 7

Ingredients:

- 1 tablespoon curry powder
- 1 teaspoon turmeric
- 1/4 cup lemon juice
- 1 can full-fat coconut milk
- 1/2 teaspoon lemon zest
- 1/2 teaspoon salt
- 4-pounds chicken breast, skin removed

Directions:

1. In a mixing bowl, mix the lemon juice, coconut milk, curry powder, turmeric, lemon zest, and salt.
2. Take an Instant Pot; open the top lid.
3. Add the chicken and bowl mix in the cooking pot. Using a spatula, gently stir to combine well.
4. Close the top lid and make sure the valve is sealed.
5. Press "POULTRY" cooking function with default cooking time.
6. Allow pressure to build and cook the ingredients for the set time.
7. After the set cooking time ends, press "CANCEL" and then press "NPR". Instant Pot will slowly and naturally release the pressure for 8-10 minutes.
8. Open the top lid, add the cooked mixture in serving plates.
9. Serve warm.

Nutritional Values (Per Serving):

Calories – 133

Fat – 11g

Carbohydrates – 8g

Fiber – 1.5g

Sodium - 295mg

Protein – 6.5g

Garlic Salsa Chicken

Prep Time: 8-10 min.

Cooking Time: 25 min.

Number of Servings: 5-6

Freestyle Points per Serving: 0

Ingredients:

- 1/8 teaspoon oregano
- Salt as needed
- ¼ teaspoon garlic powder
- 1 ½ pound skinless chicken tenders
- 1/8 teaspoon ground cumin
- 16 ounces roasted salsa verde

Directions:

1. Mix the oregano, garlic powder, salt, and cumin in a mixing bowl.
2. Coat the chicken with the prepared mix and set aside for 30 minutes to season.
3. Take an Instant Pot; open the top lid.
4. Add the seasoned chicken and salsa in the cooking pot. Using a spatula, gently stir to combine well.
5. Close the top lid and make sure the valve is sealed.
6. Press "MANUAL" cooking function. Adjust cooking time to 18-20 minutes.
7. Allow pressure to build and cook the ingredients for the set time.
8. After the set cooking time ends, press "CANCEL" and then press "QPR". Instant Pot will quickly release pressure.
9. Open the top lid, shred the chicken; add the cooked mixture in serving plates.
10. Serve warm.

Nutritional Values (Per Serving):

Calories – 153

Fat – 2.5g

Carbohydrates – 6g

Mexican Bean Chicken

Prep Time: 8-10 min.

Cooking Time: 25-30 min.

Number of Servings: 4

Freestyle Points per Serving: 6

Ingredients:

- 1 teaspoon garlic powder
- ½ teaspoon paprika
- 2 teaspoons chili powder
- 1 teaspoon cumin
- ¼ teaspoon black pepper
- ¼ teaspoon salt
- 1 green pepper, make slices
- 1 red pepper, make slices
- 1 tablespoon olive oil
- 1 pound boneless and skinless chicken breasts, make slices
- ½ onion, make slices
- 2 cups tomatoes, chopped
- 1 can black beans, rinsed and drained
- 1 cup white rice
- 1 ½ cups chicken broth

Directions:

1. Take a mixing bowl (either medium or large size), add in the chili powder, cumin, garlic powder, oregano, paprika, black pepper, and salt in the bowl to mix well with each other.
2. Take a skillet or saucepan (medium size preferable); heat it over a medium cooking flame.
3. Add the chicken and half of the spice mix; heat it.
4. Cook to evenly brown the chicken; add the remaining ingredients and season with the remaining spice mix.
5. Cover it. Let the mix simmer for about 25 minutes or until the rice cooks well.
6. Serve warm.

Nutritional Values (Per Serving):

Calories – 523

Fat – 11g

Saturated Fats – 1g

Trans Fats - 0g

Carbohydrates – 32g

Fiber – 12g

Sodium – 623mg

Protein – 42g

Cheese Cream Chicken

Prep Time: 8-10 min.

Cooking Time: 25-30 min.

Number of Servings: 6

Freestyle Points per Serving: 5

Ingredients:

- 1 (8-ounce) package biscuits
- 1/3 cup light sour cream
- ¼ cup ranch dressing
- 4 ounce light cream cheese
- 2 cups cooked shredded chicken
- 5 slices bacon, cooked and crumbled
- ½ cup low-fat cheese, shredded

Directions:

1. Preheat an oven to 375°F. Grease a baking pan (9x13) with a cooking spray.
2. Crush the biscuits; arrange over the baking pan.
3. Take a mixing bowl (either medium or large size), add in the cream cheese, sour cream, ranch dressing and chicken in the bowl to mix well with each other.
4. Add the mix over the biscuits and spread evenly.
5. Bake for 30 minutes. Serve warm.

Nutritional Values (Per Serving):

Calories – 263

Fat – 17g

Saturated Fats – 9g

Trans Fats - 0g

Carbohydrates – 18g

Fiber – 1g

Sodium – 742mg

Protein – 11g

Chicken Veggie Rice

Prep Time: 8-10 min.

Cooking Time: 15 min.

Number of Servings: 6

Freestyle Points per Serving: 2

Ingredients:

- 1 onion, chopped
- 2 cloves of garlic, minced
- 1 teaspoon olive oil
- 4 large egg whites
- 12 ounces skinless chicken breasts make ½" cubes
- 2 cups long-grain brown rice, cooked
- 3 tablespoons soy sauce, low-sodium
- ½ cups carrots, chopped
- ½ cup frozen green peas

Directions:

1. Take a skillet or saucepan (medium size preferable); heat it over a medium cooking flame.
2. Add the oil and heat it.
3. Add the egg whites and cook until scrambled. Set it aside.
4. Add and cook the onions, garlic, and chicken breasts for 5-6 minutes until lightly brown. Add the carrots and peas.
5. Cook for 2-3 more minutes.
6. Stir in the rice and soy sauce. Add the cooked egg mix and stir-cook for 2-3 more minutes.
7. Serve warm.

Nutritional Values (Per Serving):

Calories – 142

Fat – 3g

Saturated Fats – 1g

Trans Fats - 0g

Carbohydrates – 21g

Fiber – 2g

Sodium – 642mg

Protein – 23g

Turkey Apple Patties

Prep Time: 8-10 min.

Cooking Time: 10 min.

Number of Servings: 4

Freestyle Points per Serving: 1

Ingredients:

- 1 tablespoon sage, minced
- 2 teaspoons Dijon mustard
- 1 green apple, cored and grated
- 1-pound lean skinless ground turkey
- ½ teaspoon salt
- ¼ teaspoon onion powder
- 2 teaspoons olive oil
- ¼ teaspoon pepper
- ¼ teaspoon garlic powder

Directions:

1. Take a mixing bowl (either medium or large size), add in the ingredients except for the olive oil in the bowl to mix well with each other.
2. Make 4 patties and add in your fridge for 30 minutes before cooking.
3. Take a skillet or saucepan (medium size preferable); heat it over a medium cooking flame.
4. Add the oil and heat it.
5. Cook the patties on both the sides until turning brown for 4-5 minutes.
6. Serve with green veggies or salad mix.

Nutritional Values (Per Serving):

Calories – 137

Fat – 3g

Saturated Fats – 0g

Trans Fats - 0g

Carbohydrates – 25g

Fiber – 4g

Sodium – 37mg

Protein – 6g

Marinara Cheese Chicken

Prep Time: 8-10 min.

Cooking Time: 20 min.

Number of Servings: 4

Freestyle Points per Serving: 5

Ingredients:

- ¼ cup panko breadcrumbs
- ¼ cup grated parmesan cheese
- Pepper and salt as per taste
- 1 teaspoon garlic powder
- 1 teaspoon Italian seasoning
- 1-pound boneless chicken cutlets, skins removed
- 1 egg, whisked
- 3 cups green beans
- 2 teaspoons olive oil
- ½ cup marinara sauce
- ¼ cup basil, chopped
- ½ cup mozzarella cheese

Directions:

1. Preheat an oven to 425°F.
2. Take a mixing bowl (either medium or large size), add in the breadcrumbs, parmesan cheese, garlic powder, seasoning, salt, and pepper in the bowl to mix well with each other.
3. Take a mixing bowl (either medium or large size), crack and whisk the eggs.
4. Add and coat the breasts into the egg and coat with the breadcrumb mixture.
5. Take a baking sheet and coat with olive oil. Spread the beans over it and then arrange the chicken breasts over the baking sheet.
6. Cook for 15 minutes or until the chicken is cooked well.
7. Add the marinara sauce and cheese on top. Add to the oven and bake for 5 minutes. Top with the basil and serve warm.

Nutritional Values (Per Serving):

Calories - 457

Fat – 12g

Saturated Fats – 6g

Trans Fats - 0g

Carbohydrates – 37g

Fiber – 9g

Sodium – 842mg

Protein – 27g

Turkey Bean Chili

Prep Time: 8-10 min.

Cooking Time: 25 min.

Number of Servings: 4

Freestyle Points per Serving: 1

Ingredients:

- 2 cloves of garlic, minced
- 1 red pepper, chopped
- ½ cup celery, chopped
- ½ tablespoon olive oil
- 1 onion, chopped
- 1 jalapeno pepper, seeded and cut to dice
- 1 ½ tablespoon chili powder
- 1 teaspoon oregano
- 2 tablespoons chipotle pepper, cut to dice
- 1-pound lean ground turkey meat
- 1 teaspoon ground cumin
- 1 bay leaf
- Pepper and salt as per taste
- 1 can kidney beans, rinsed and drained
- 1 cup tomatoes, cut to dice
- ¾ cup chicken broth, low sodium

Directions:

1. Take a skillet or saucepan (medium size preferable); heat it over a medium cooking flame.
2. Add the oil and heat it.
3. Add and stir cook the onion, garlic, red pepper, celery, jalapeno, and chipotle for 4-5 minutes.
4. Mix in the turkey, chili powder, oregano, and ground cumin; cook for another 5 minutes.
5. Add the rest of the ingredients; mix and simmer for 20 minutes. Serve warm.

Nutritional Values (Per Serving):

Calories – 186

Fat – 3g

Saturated Fats – 0g

Trans Fats - 0g

Carbohydrates – 26g

Fiber – 7g

Sodium – 532mg

Protein – 11g

Orange Pineapple Chicken

Prep Time: 8-10 min.

Cooking Time: 12 min.

Number of Servings: 8

Freestyle Points per Serving: 1

Ingredients:

- ¼ cup soy sauce
- 1 teaspoon garlic powder
- 1-pound skinless chicken breasts, make 2-inch chunks
- ½ cup orange juice
- 1 teaspoon onion powder
- ½ teaspoon ginger
- ½ yellow bell pepper, seeded and cubed
- ½ red bell pepper, seeded and cubed
- 1 teaspoon black pepper
- 1 teaspoon salt
- ½ red onion, make wedges
- 1 ½ cups pineapple, make slices

Directions:

1. Take a mixing bowl (either medium or large size), add in the chicken, orange juice, soy sauce, garlic powder, onion powder, black pepper, salt and ginger in the bowl to mix well with each other.
2. Place to marinate for 2 hours inside the fridge.
3. Take the skewers. Skew the bell pepper, onions, and pineapple, and chicken onto them in altering manner.
4. Heat the grill to high-temperature setting; cook the skewers for 5-6 minutes on each side until cooks well.
5. Serve warm.

Nutritional Values (Per Serving):

Calories – 238

Fat – 1g

Saturated Fats – 0g

Trans Fats - 0g

Carbohydrates – 34g

Fiber – 5g

Sodium – 723mg

Protein – 20g

BBQ Turkey Meatballs

Prep Time: 8-10 min.

Cooking Time: 15-20 min.

Number of Servings: 5-6

Freestyle Points per Serving: 1

Ingredients:

- 1 teaspoon black pepper
- 1 teaspoon onion powder
- 1-pound ground skinless turkey breasts
- ½ teaspoon salt
- 1 teaspoon garlic powder
- ¼ cup teriyaki sauce
- ¼ cup BBQ sauce, sugar-free
- 1 teaspoon paprika
- 1 teaspoon cumin
- 1/3 cup apple cider vinegar
- 1 tablespoon brown sugar

Directions:

1. Take a mixing bowl (either medium or large size), add in the dry ingredients except for the sugar in the bowl to mix well with each other. Form into 12 meatballs.
2. In another bowl, combine the wet ingredients and sugar.
3. Preheat an oven to 375°F.
4. Bake the meatballs for 8-10 minutes.
5. Turn the meatballs and cook for 10 more minutes.
6. Serve with the sauce mix.

Nutritional Values (Per Serving):

Calories – 281

Fat – 1g

Saturated Fats – 0g

Trans Fats - 0g

Carbohydrates – 43g

Fiber – 6g

Sodium – 532mg

Protein – 16g

Chicken Mushroom Meatballs

Prep Time: 8-10 min.

Cooking Time: 25-30 min.

Number of Servings: 9-10

Freestyle Points per Serving: 5

Ingredients:

- 1/3 cup whole wheat bread crumbs
- ¼ cup pecorino cheese, grated
- 8 ounces cremini mushrooms, chopped finely
- 1-pound lean ground chicken
- 1 large egg, beaten
- 1 teaspoon salt
- 2 tablespoons chopped parsley
- 3 cloves of garlic, minced
- A dash of black pepper
- ½ tablespoon all-purpose flour
- ½ tablespoon unsalted butter
- ¼ cup shallots, chopped
- 1/3 cup Marsala wine
- ¾ cup chicken broth, low sodium
- 3 ounces shiitake mushrooms, make slices

Directions:

1. Preheat an oven to 400°F.
2. Take a mixing bowl (either medium or large size), add in the mushrooms, chicken, bread crumbs, cheese, egg, parsley, garlic, salt, and pepper in the bowl to mix well with each other.
3. Form small meatballs and arrange in a greased baking sheet. Bake for 20 minutes and set aside.
4. Take a mixing bowl (either medium or large size), add in the flour, Marsala wine, and broth in the bowl to mix well with each other.
5. Take a skillet or saucepan (medium size preferable); heat it over a medium cooking flame.

6. Add the butter and heat it.
7. Add and sauté the shallots until fragrant. Stir in the mushrooms and cook for 2-3 minutes.
8. Pour in the broth mix; simmer for 5 minutes until the mix thickens.
9. Serve meatballs with the sauce.

Nutritional Values (Per Serving):

Calories – 82

Fat – 3g

Saturated Fats – 1g

Trans Fats - 0g

Carbohydrates – 6g

Fiber – 1g

Sodium – 423mg

Protein – 5g

Turkey Vegetable Mix

Prep Time: 8-10 min.

Cooking Time: 5 min.

Number of Servings: 4

Freestyle Points per Serving: 2

Ingredients:

- 4 tablespoon soy sauce
- 2 minced cloves of garlic
- 2 tablespoon minced ginger
- 2 tablespoon rice vinegar
- 1 (16 ounce) bag vegetable mix (broccoli, carrot, spinach, etc.)
- 1 pound ground turkey (99% lean)
- 1 tablespoon sesame oil
- 1 tablespoon coconut oil

Directions:

1. Take a skillet or saucepan (medium size preferable); heat it over a medium cooking flame.
2. Add the oil and heat it.
3. Add the turkey, garlic, and ginger; stir cook until the turkey cooks well.
4. Add the veggies and cook for 4-5 more minutes.
5. Mix in the soy sauce and vinegar. Cook for 1-2 more minutes.
6. Season as needed and serve warm.

Nutritional Values (Per Serving):

Calories – 286

Fat – 14g

Saturated Fats – 6g

Trans Fats - 0g

Carbohydrates – 16g

Fiber – 3g

Sodium – 712mg

Protein – 24g

Chapter 5: Freestyle Red Meat

Zucchini Chili Beef

Prep Time: 8-10 min.

Cooking Time: 20 min.

Number of Servings: 4

Freestyle Points per Serving: 6

Ingredients:

- 3 minced garlic cloves
- 1 pound lean ground beef
- 1 teaspoon olive oil
- 1 chopped onion
- 1 can (4 ounce) green chilies
- 1 lime, juiced
- 1 tablespoon chili powder
- 1 can (14 ounce) tomatoes, diced
- 1 can (14 ounce) black beans, drained
- 2 chopped zucchinis
- Ground black pepper & salt as per taste

Directions:

1. Take a skillet or saucepan (medium size preferable); heat it over a medium cooking flame.
2. Add the oil and heat it.
3. Add the onions and garlic. Sauté for 2-3 minutes to make them soft and add the beef.
4. Cook until turns even brown; stir in the chilies, beans, tomatoes, lime juice, chili powder, pepper, and salt.
5. Continue cooking for 8-10 minutes; add the zucchini. Cook 8-10 more minutes and serve warm.

Nutritional Values (Per Serving):

Calories – 374

Fat – 14g

Saturated Fats – 5g

Trans Fats - 0g

Carbohydrates – 27g

Fiber – 10g

Sodium – 237mg

Protein – 31g

Beef Lettuce Burgers

Prep Time: 8-10 min.

Cooking Time: 10 min.

Number of Servings: 4

Freestyle Points per Serving: 4

Ingredients:

- ½ teaspoon salt
- 1 tablespoon Worcestershire sauce
- 2 teaspoons garlic, minced
- ¼ teaspoon pepper
- 4 hamburger buns, low calorie
- 1 pound ground beef
- Shredded lettuce as needed

Directions:

1. Coat a griddle with some olive oil or cooking spray and heat it.
2. Take a mixing bowl (either medium or large size), add in the pepper, salt, Worcestershire sauce, garlic, and beef in the bowl to mix well with each other.
3. Prepare 4 patties from the mix.
4. Place them over the griddle and cook for 4-5 minutes on each side.
5. Take the buns and make burgers with your favorite toppings, lettuce, and serve.

Nutritional Values (Per Serving):

Calories – 327

Fat – 12g

Saturated Fats – 5g

Trans Fats - 0g

Carbohydrates – 22g

Fiber – 1g

Sodium – 642mg

Protein – 27g

Creamy Pork Chops

Prep Time: 8-10 min.

Cooking Time: 15 min.

Number of Servings: 4

Freestyle Points per Serving: 5

Ingredients:

- 4 pork loin chops, center-cut
- 1/3 cup non-fat, half-and-half
- 1/3 cup fat-free chicken stock
- 1/2 teaspoon salt
- 1 1/2 tablespoon Dijon mustard
- 1/2 teaspoon black pepper
- 1/2 teaspoon onion powder
- Pinch of dried thyme

Directions:

1. Rub the salt, pepper, and onion powder over the chops.
2. Take a skillet or saucepan (medium size preferable); heat it over a medium cooking flame.
3. Add the oil and heat it.
4. Add the meat and cook, while stirring, until turns evenly brown for 3-4 minute per side.
5. Pour the stock, mustard, and half-and-half.
6. Lower temperature setting; cook for 6-7 more minutes.
7. When the sauce becomes thick, add the thyme. Serve warm.

Nutritional Values (Per Serving):

Calories – 134

Fat – 5g

Saturated Fats – 2g

Trans Fats - 0g

Carbohydrates – 2g

Fiber – 0g

Sodium – 447mg

Protein – 14g

Beef Broccoli Dinner

Prep Time: 8-10 min.

Cooking Time: 10-15 min.

Number of Servings: 4

Freestyle Points per Serving: 3

Ingredients:

- 3/4 pound lean sirloin beef
- 1/4 teaspoon salt
- 5 cups broccoli florets
- 1 cup chicken broth, reduced-sodium
- 2 ½ tablespoon cornstarch
- 2 teaspoon canola oil
- 1/4 cup water
- 1/4 teaspoon red pepper flakes
- 2 tablespoon minced garlic
- 1/4 cup soy sauce
- 1 tablespoon minced ginger root

Directions:

1. Combine the 2 tablespoons cornstarch and salt; coat the beef with it.
2. Take a skillet or saucepan (medium size preferable); heat it over a medium cooking flame.
3. Add the oil and heat it.
4. Add the beef and cook, while stirring, until turns evenly brown for 3-4 minutes. Set the beef aside.
5. Add ½ cup of the broth, broccoli and cook for 2-3 minutes.
6. Add the garlic, ginger, and pepper flakes. Simmer the mix for 1 more minute.
7. Take a mixing bowl (either medium or large size), add in the rest of the broth, soy sauce, and rest of the cornstarch in the bowl to mix well with each other.
8. Turn down heat; cover and simmer for 1 minute. Mix in the broth mix and beef; serve warm.

Nutritional Values (Per Serving):

Calories – 253

Fat – 11g

Saturated Fats – 3g

Trans Fats - 0g

Carbohydrates – 7g

Fiber – 1g

Sodium – 753mg

Protein – 27g

Roast Taco Wraps

Prep Time: 8-10 min.

Cooking Time: 0 min.

Number of Servings: 7

Freestyle Points per Serving: 6

Ingredients:

- ½ pound cooked roast beef, make slices
- 2 make slices tomatoes
- ¼ teaspoon pepper
- 7 pieces tortilla
- 2 teaspoon Dijon mustard
- 1/3 cup basil
- 1/3 cup mayo
- 2 cup shredded lettuce
- ¼ teaspoon salt

Directions:

1. Take a mixing bowl (either medium or large size), add in the pepper, mustard, salt, basil, and mayo in the bowl to mix well with each other.
2. Arrange the tortillas and spread the mix; top with some lettuce, roast beef, and tomatoes. Roll the tortillas and serve.

Nutritional Values (Per Serving):

Calories – 193

Fat – 9g

Saturated Fats – 2g

Trans Fats - 0g

Carbohydrates – 16g

Fiber – 1g

Sodium – 647mg

Protein – 12g

Grilled Spiced Chops

Prep Time: 8-10 min.

Cooking Time: 8 min.

Number of Servings: 4

Freestyle Points per Serving: 6

Ingredients:

- 2 teaspoons brown sugar
- 1 1/3 pound boneless pork chops
- 2 teaspoons vegetable oil
- 2 teaspoons sweet paprika
- 1/2 teaspoon ground garlic powder
- 1/2 teaspoon ground cinnamon
- 1/2 teaspoon kosher salt
- 1/2 teaspoon ground ginger

Directions:

1. Take a mixing bowl (either medium or large size), add in the paprika, sugar, chili powder, cinnamon, salt, ginger, and garlic powder in the bowl to mix well with each other.
2. Rub over the chops.
3. Preheat your grill over medium-high temperature setting.
4. Grill 3-4 minutes for each side; until cooks well.
5. Serve warm.

Nutritional Values (Per Serving):

Calories – 367

Fat – 23g

Saturated Fats – 3g

Trans Fats - 0g

Carbohydrates – 3g

Fiber – 0g

Sodium – 283mg

Protein – 36g

Avocado Crab Salad

Prep Time: 8-10 min.

Cooking Time: 0 min.

Number of Servings: 2

Freestyle Points per Serving: 5

Ingredients:

- 2 teaspoons Asian hot sauce
- 1 teaspoon fresh chives
- 2 teaspoons low-fat mayo
- 4-ounce crabmeat, chopped
- 1/4 cup cucumber, diced

For the Avocado:

- 1 small ripe avocado, pitted and sliced
- 2 teaspoon soy sauce
- 1/2 teaspoon sesame seeds

Directions:

1. Take a mixing bowl (either medium or large size), add in the ingredients except for the soy sauce and sesame seeds in the bowl to mix well with each other.
2. Top with the sauce and seeds; serve.

Nutritional Values (Per Serving):

Calories – 178

Fat – 12g

Saturated Fats – 2g

Trans Fats - 0g

Carbohydrates – 11g

Fiber – 5g

Sodium – 563mg

Protein – 13g

Potato Mayo Fish

Prep Time: 8-10 min.

Cooking Time: 12 min.

Number of Servings: 3

Freestyle Points per Serving: 4

Ingredients:

- ½ teaspoon lemon juice
- ½ teaspoon ground mustard
- 3 tablespoons light mayonnaise
- ½ teaspoon pickle relish
- 2 tablespoons green onions, chopped
- Pepper and salt as per taste
- ½ cup butter, melted
- 4 (3-ounce) tilapia fillet
- ½ cup potato flakes

Directions:

1. Preheat an oven to 450°F.
2. Take a mixing bowl (either medium or large size), add in the mayonnaise, pickle, lemon juice, mustard, and green onions in the bowl to mix well with each other.
3. Coat the fish with the mayo mixture and then dredge on the potato flakes; pat gently and sprinkle with pepper and salt as per taste.
4. Arrange over a baking sheet and bake for 12 minutes. After 6 minutes, brush with the butter and cook for 6 more minutes. Serve warm.

Nutritional Values (Per Serving):

Calories – 533

Fat – 32g

Saturated Fats – 18g

Trans Fats - 0g

Carbohydrates – 6g

Fiber – 1g

Sodium – 654mg

Protein – 13g

Tuna Cranberry Salad

Prep Time: 8-10 min.

Cooking Time: 0 min.

Number of Servings: 5

Freestyle Points per Serving: 3

Ingredients:

Seasoning:

- Red pepper flakes, black pepper, sea salt as needed

Salad:

- 3 tablespoons light sour cream
- 1 can (16 ounce) white tuna in spring water
- 3 tables low-fat mayonnaise
- 1/4 cup red onion, minced
- 1 tablespoon lemon juice
- 1 cored apple, sliced
- 1/4 cup dried cranberries
- 1/2 cup celery, chopped

Directions:

1. Take a mixing bowl (either medium or large size), add in the salad ingredients in the bowl to mix well with each other.
2. Season as needed and serve.

Nutritional Values (Per Serving):

Calories – 83

Fat – 1g

Saturated Fats – 0g

Trans Fats - 0g

Carbohydrates – 13g

Fiber – 2g

Sodium – 164mg

Protein – 4g

Salmon Asparagus Treat

Prep Time: 8-10 min.

Cooking Time: 15 min.

Number of Servings: 4

Freestyle Points per Serving: 4

Ingredients:

- 2 tablespoons lemon juice
- 1/2 teaspoon oregano
- 4 salmon fillets
- 2 tablespoons Dijon mustard
- 1/2 teaspoon dried dill
- pepper and salt as needed
- 1 pound asparagus
- 1 pound thinly sliced sweet potatoes
- 2 minced garlic cloves
- 1 tablespoon olive oil

Directions:

1. Preheat an oven to 450°F.
2. Take a mixing bowl (either medium or large size), add in the oregano, half of the garlic, lemon juice, dill, and mustard in the bowl to mix well with each other.
3. Arrange the fillets in the pan and brush with the sauce.
4. Combine the salt, pepper, oil, and rest of the garlic in another mixing bowl.
5. Mix in the asparagus and potato slices.
6. Arrange the vegetables in a greased baking pan and bake for 12-15 minutes until the fish is flaky.
7. Serve warm.

Nutritional Values (Per Serving):

Calories – 327

Fat – 14g

Saturated Fats – 2g

Trans Fats - 0g

Carbohydrates – 23g

Fiber – 5g

Sodium – 163mg

Protein – 26g

Baked Spiced Fish

Prep Time: 8-10 min.

Cooking Time: 10 min.

Number of Servings: 4-5

Freestyle Points per Serving: 2

Ingredients:

- ½ teaspoon salt
- 3 tablespoon melted butter
- ½ teaspoon paprika
- 1/3 cup milk
- 1/8 teaspoon pepper
- 1 ½ pound white fish fillet
- ¼ cup yellow cornmeal
- ¼ cup breadcrumbs
- ½ teaspoon dill

Directions:

1. Preheat an oven to 450°F.
2. Take a mixing bowl (either medium or large size), add in the dry ingredients in the bowl to mix well with each other.
3. Add in the milk in another bowl and dip the fish coat and then coat with the crumb mixture.
4. Add into a greased pan and top with some melted butter.
5. Bake the fish for 8-10 minutes and then serve with your favorite sides.

Nutritional Values (Per Serving):

Calories – 223

Fat – 9g

Saturated Fats – 5g

Trans Fats - 0g

Carbohydrates – 28g

Fiber – 3g

Sodium – 85mg

Protein – 7g

Cod Shrimp Stew

Prep Time: 8-10 min.

Cooking Time: 35 min.

Number of Servings: 6

Freestyle Points per Serving: 2

Ingredients:

- 28 ounce canned tomatoes
- 3 tablespoons tomato paste
- 8 ounce clam juice
- 1 cut to dice onion
- 1 tablespoon olive oil
- 2 minced garlic cloves
- 2 tablespoons butter
- 2/3 cup parsley
- 14 ounce fish stock
- 1/2 teaspoon Basil
- 1/4 teaspoon red pepper flakes
- Pepper and salt to taste
- 1/2 teaspoon oregano
- 1 pound raw shrimp
- 1.5 pound cod, make small pieces

Directions:

1. Take a skillet or saucepan (medium size preferable); heat it over medium cooking flame.
2. Add the oil and heat it.
3. Add and cook the onions to soften for 5-6 minutes.
4. Stir in the flakes and garlic.
5. Cook for 1-2 minutes. Mix in the paste and cook for 1-2 minute.
6. Mix in the stock, clam juice and tomatoes; simmer the mix and mix in the butter, oregano, and basil.
7. Simmer the mix for 10-15 more minutes. Add the fish and cook for 4-5 minutes; mix in the shrimp and cook for 3-4 more minutes. Serve warm.

Nutritional Values (Per Serving):

Calories – 343

Fat – 12g

Saturated Fats – 4g

Trans Fats - 0g

Carbohydrates – 14g

Fiber – 2g

Sodium – 1147mg

Protein – 36g

Shrimp Blue Cheese Salad

Prep Time: 8-10 min.

Cooking Time: 5 min.

Number of Servings: 2

Freestyle Points per Serving: 7

Ingredients:

- 4 ounce lettuce, chopped
- 2 cloves garlic, minced
- 1/2 pound shrimp, peeled and deveined
- 4 slices bacon, center-cut, chopped
- 2 teaspoon olive oil
- ½ cup halved cherry tomatoes
- 1 ounce blue cheese
- 2 ounce avocado, pitted and diced
- Black pepper and salt to taste
- 1 small corn on the cob, grilled or roasted

Directions:

1. Take a skillet or saucepan (medium size preferable); heat it over medium cooking flame.
2. Add the bacon and cook to crisp evenly. Discard the grease and set aside.
3. Add the shrimp and garlic; cook for 2-3 minutes until it becomes opaque.
4. Remove and chop it into bite-sized pieces. Season as needed and top with the olive oil. Serve warm.

Nutritional Values (Per Serving):

Calories – 324

Fat – 21g

Saturated Fats – 5g

Trans Fats - 0g

Carbohydrates – 17g

Fiber – 5g

Sodium – 734mg

Protein – 36g

Chapter 7: Freestyle Meatless Recipes

Potato Buttermilk Appetizer

Prep Time: 8-10 min.

Cooking Time: 12 min.

Number of Servings: 6

Freestyle Points per Serving: 4

Ingredients:

- 1/3 cup buttermilk, low-fat
- ½ teaspoon kosher salt
- ¼ cup sour cream
- 3 cups water
- 2-pound russet potatoes, peeled and make quarters
- 1 teaspoon salt
- 2 tablespoons butter
- Parsley as required, chopped
- Black pepper as needed

Directions:

1. Take an Instant Pot; open the top lid.
2. Add the water, salt, and potato in the cooking pot. Using a spatula, gently stir to combine well.
3. Close the top lid and make sure the valve is sealed.
4. Press "MANUAL" cooking function. Adjust cooking time to 10-12 minutes.
5. Allow pressure to build and cook the ingredients for the set time.
6. After the set cooking time ends, press "CANCEL" and then press "QPR". Instant Pot will quickly release pressure.
7. Open the top lid, drain water except for ½ cup and add the potatoes in a blender. Add ½ cup of water also.
8. Add in the remaining ingredients and blend to create a mash like consistency.
9. Serve warm.

Nutritional Values (Per Serving):

Calories - 138

Fat – 4.5g

Carbohydrates – 26.5g

Fiber – 3g

Sodium - 312mg

Protein – 5g

Orange Glazed Potatoes

Prep Time: 8-10 min.

Cooking Time: 20 min.

Number of Servings: 7-8

Freestyle Points per Serving: 4

Ingredients:

- 1 tablespoon cinnamon
- 1 tablespoon blackstrap molasses
- ½ cup orange juice
- 4 cups sweet potatoes, make small-sized pieces
- 1 teaspoon vanilla
- ¼ cup sugar

Directions:

1. In a heat-proof bowl, add the potatoes. Mix in the cinnamon, molasses, sugar, orange juice, and vanilla.
2. Take an Instant Pot; open the top lid.
3. Pour 1 cup water and place steamer basket/trivet inside the cooking pot.
4. Arrange the bowl over the basket/trivet.
5. Close the top lid and make sure the valve is sealed.
6. Press "MANUAL" cooking function. Adjust cooking time to 20-22 minutes.
7. Allow pressure to build and cook the ingredients for the set time.
8. After the set cooking time ends, press "CANCEL" and then press "NPR". Instant Pot will slowly and naturally release the pressure for 8-10 minutes.
9. Open the top lid, add the cooked mixture in serving plates.
10. Serve warm.

Nutritional Values (Per Serving):

Calories - 112

Fat – 4.5g

Carbohydrates – 16g

Fiber – 3g

Sodium - 173mg

Protein – 3g

Broccoli Spinach Greens

Prep Time: 8-10 min.

Cooking Time: 5 min.

Number of Servings: 4-5

Freestyle Points per Serving: 1

Ingredients:

- 2 cups kale, chopped
- 1/2 teaspoon cumin, ground
- 2 cups broccoli, chopped
- 2 cups baby spinach
- 1/2 teaspoon coriander, ground
- 2 cloves garlic, crushed or minced
- 2 tablespoons coconut oil
- 1 tablespoon ginger, minced

Directions:

1. Take an Instant Pot; open the top lid.
2. Press "SAUTÉ" cooking function.
3. In the cooking pot area, add the oil, garlic, ginger, and broccoli. Cook until turn translucent and softened for 4-5 minutes.
4. Add the remaining ingredients.
5. Cook until spinach and kale are wilted.
6. Add the cooked mixture in serving plates.
7. Serve warm.

Nutritional Values (Per Serving):

Calories - 93

Fat – 5.5g

Carbohydrates – 4g

Fiber – 1g

Sodium - 33mg

Protein – 4.5g

Mango Arugula Salad

Prep Time: 8-10 min.

Cooking Time: 0 min.

Number of Servings: 4-5

Freestyle Points per Serving: 3

Ingredients:

- 4 cups baby arugula
- 3 tablespoons chopped walnuts
- 1 tablespoon vinegar, balsamic
- 1 tablespoon olive oil, extra virgin
- 3 medium ripe mangos, seeded and make slices
- ¾ cup red onion, make slices
- 1/2 tablespoon lemon juice
- 1/8 tablespoon lemon zest
- Black pepper and salt as per taste

Directions:

1. Take a mixing bowl (either medium or large size), add in the peaches, yellow pepper, arugula, and walnuts in the bowl to mix well with each other.
2. In a bowl whisk the olive oil, vinegar, lemon juice, pepper and salt and drizzle over the salad. Serve fresh.

Nutritional Values (Per Serving):

Calories – 192

Fat – 7g

Saturated Fats – 1g

Trans Fats - 0g

Carbohydrates – 33g

Fiber – 4g

Sodium – 24mg

Protein – 3g

Cream Mayo Corn

Prep Time: 8-10 min.

Cooking Time: 20 min.

Number of Servings: 8

Freestyle Points per Serving: 2

Ingredients:

- ¼ cup grated Parmesan cheese
- ½ cup Greek yogurt, plain and non-fat
- 16-ounce bag frozen sweet corn on the cob
- ½ cup fat-free mayonnaise
- ½ teaspoon cayenne pepper
- Pepper and salt as per taste

Directions:

1. Take a mixing bowl (either medium or large size), add in all the ingredients in the bowl to mix well with each other.
2. Preheat your grill over high-temperature setting.
3. Arrange the corn ears in a cooking pan and cover with a foil. Grill for 18-20 minutes.
4. Serve warm.

Nutritional Values (Per Serving):

Calories – 272

Fat – 16g

Saturated Fats – 9g

Trans Fats - 0g

Carbohydrates – 9g

Fiber – 2g

Sodium – 961mg

Protein – 22g

Eggs Green Bean Salad

Prep Time: 8-10 min.

Cooking Time: 10-15 min.

Number of Servings: 7-8

Freestyle Points per Serving: 3

Ingredients:

- 3 ounce olives, sliced
- 2 eggs, hard-boiled, peeled and diced
- 24 ounces green beans, ends trimmed
- ¼ cup olive oil, extra virgin
- Salt and fresh pepper as needed
- ¼ cup balsamic vinegar
- 3 scallions, chopped up

Directions:

1. Steam the beans in a large pot with boiling water until cooked well. Drain water and cool down the beans.
2. Take a mixing bowl (either medium or large size), add in the balsamic, oil, pepper and salt in the bowl to mix well with each other.
3. Mix in the olives, scallions, and beans.
4. Top with the eggs and serve.

Nutritional Values (Per Serving):

Calories – 386

Fat – 32g

Saturated Fats – 5g

Trans Fats - 0g

Carbohydrates – 27g

Fiber – 2g

Sodium – 322mg

Protein – 3g

Feta Chickpea Salad

Prep Time: 8-10 min.

Cooking Time: 0 min.

Number of Servings: 4

Freestyle Points per Serving: 6

Ingredients:

- 2 cup diced, cucumber
- 15 ounce can chickpeas, drained and rinsed
- 4 ounce feta, make slices or crumbled
- 20 kalamata olives
- 1 green bell pepper, make slices
- 1 1/3 cup grape tomatoes, halved
- 1/4 cup red onion, make slices

For the dressing:

- Juice of 2 lemons
- 2 tablespoons olive oil, extra virgin
- 1/4 teaspoon kosher salt
- 2 teaspoons oregano leaves, minced-up
- Ground black pepper as needed

Directions:

1. Take a mixing bowl (either medium or large size), add in the chickpeas, cucumber, green pepper, tomato, olives, and red onion in the bowl to mix well with each other.
2. Mix in the cheese.
3. In another bowl, mix the oil, lemon juice, oregano, pepper, and salt in it. Whisk thoroughly.
4. Serve the salad with the lemon mix.

Nutritional Values (Per Serving):

Calories – 438

Fat – 17g

Saturated Fats – 5g

Trans Fats - 0g

Carbohydrates – 57g

Fiber – 16g

Sodium – 463mg

Protein – 19g

Feta Corn Treat

Prep Time: 8-10 min.

Cooking Time: 12 min.

Number of Servings: 6

Freestyle Points per Serving: 3

Ingredients:

- ¼ cup chopped, red onion
- 2 tablespoons worth of olive oil, extra virgin
- 7 medium ears of corn
- ½ cup feta cheese, crumbled
- 3 tablespoons chopped, mint
- Black pepper as per taste
- ¼ teaspoon salt

Directions:

1. Grill the corn on the preheated grill for 10-12 minute while turning.
2. Cool down and remove the kernels off the cob.
3. Take a mixing bowl (either medium or large size), add in the red onion, cheese, and corn in the bowl to mix well with each other.
4. Mix in the olive oil and herbs; season and serve.

Nutritional Values (Per Serving):

Calories – 286

Fat – 14g

Saturated Fats – 6g

Trans Fats - 0g

Carbohydrates – 41g

Fiber – 5g

Sodium – 642mg

Protein – 9g

Marinara Broccoli Meal

Prep Time: 8-10 min.

Cooking Time: 30 min.

Number of Servings: 3

Freestyle Points per Serving: 4

Ingredients:

- 2 tablespoons olive oil, extra virgin
- ½ teaspoon salt
- 1 medium bunch of broccoli, make small florets
- 6 cloves garlic, peeled and smashed
- 1 cup marinara sauce
- ½ cup parmesan cheese, shredded

Directions:

1. Preheat an oven to 450°F.
2. Arrange the broccoli and garlic cloves on a baking pan and drizzle with the olive oil.
3. Season with salt and bake for 8-10 minutes to evenly brown the broccoli.
4. Turn the broccoli and garlic and roast for 10 more minutes.
5. Top with marinara sauce and cheese; bake for 8 more minutes and serve warm.

Nutritional Values (Per Serving):

Calories – 537

Fat – 34g

Saturated Fats – 18g

Trans Fats - 0g

Carbohydrates – 9g

Fiber – 1g

Sodium – 845mg

Protein – 34g

Arugula Greens Salad

Prep Time: 8-10 min.

Cooking Time: 0 min.

Number of Servings: 8-10

Freestyle Points per Serving: 6

Ingredients:

- 2 ounce pecans, chopped
- 1 cup pomegranate seeds
- 5 cups mixed baby greens
- 5 cups bunch baby arugula
- ½ cup gorgonzola cheese, crumbled

For the dressing:

- 3 tablespoons champagne vinegar
- Pepper and salt as needed
- 5 tablespoons olive oil, extra virgin
- 1 tablespoon honey
- 5 tablespoons pomegranate juice, unsweetened
- 1 tablespoon shallots, finely minced

Directions:

1. Take a mixing bowl (either medium or large size), add in the pomegranate juice, vinegar, salt, honey, olive oil, and pepper in the bowl to mix well with each other. Set aside.
2. Mix the mixed greens in another bowl. Mix the remaining ingredients and top with the dressing.

Nutritional Values (Per Serving):

Calories – 226

Fat – 19g

Saturated Fats – 5g

Trans Fats - 0g

Carbohydrates – 11g

Fiber – 2g

Sodium – 562mg

Protein – 6g

Egg Mayo Salad

Prep Time: 8-10 min.

Cooking Time: 15-20 min.

Number of Servings: 2-3

Freestyle Points per Serving: 2

Ingredients:

- 1 piece of dill
- 2 tablespoons mayo
- ¼ teaspoon pepper
- ½ teaspoon salt
- ½ teaspoon Dijon mustard
- 2 hard-boiled eggs, diced
- 2 tablespoons chives

Directions:

1. Take a mixing bowl (either medium or large size), add in the ingredients in the bowl to mix well with each other.
2. Serve fresh.

Nutritional Values (Per Serving):

Calories – 154

Fat – 11g

Saturated Fats – 3g

Trans Fats - 0g

Carbohydrates – 2g

Fiber – 0g

Sodium – 657mg

Protein – 11g

Blueberry Lemon Muffins

Prep Time: 8-10 min.

Cooking Time: 25 min.

Number of Servings: 15

Freestyle Points per Serving: 5

Ingredients:

- 2 teaspoons pure lemon extract
- 3 tablespoons lemon juice
- 1 ¼ cups blueberries
- 1 teaspoon vanilla extract
- 1/3 cup canola oil
- ½ cup sugar
- 1 ½ cups whole wheat flour
- 1 cup soy milk, unsweetened
- ½ teaspoon salt
- 2 teaspoons baking soda
- 1 teaspoon apple cider vinegar

Directions:

1. Take 15 muffin tins and line them with liner. Preheat an oven to 350°F.
2. Take a mixing bowl (either medium or large size), add and mix in the vanilla extract, lemon extract, lemon juice, canola oil, salt, baking soda, soy milk, and vinegar in the bowl to mix well with each other.
3. Stir in the sugar and mix well. Stir in the flour and mix well; now mix in the blueberries.
4. Add the mix in the prepared muffin tins.
5. Bake for 22-25 minutes until tops are lightly browned and cooked through.

Nutritional Values (Per Serving):

Calories – 124

Fat – 6g

Saturated Fats – 0g

Trans Fats - 0g

Carbohydrates – 19g

Fiber – 2g

Sodium – 347mg

Protein – 1g

Applesauce Bean Brownies

Prep Time: 8-10 min.

Cooking Time: 30-35 min.

Number of Servings: 12

Freestyle Points per Serving: 1

Ingredients:

- ¼ cup all-purpose flour
- 1/3 cup unsweetened cocoa powder
- ½ teaspoon baking powder
- ½ teaspoon salt
- ¼ cup applesauce, unsweetened
- 1 ½ cups black beans
- ¼ cup blackstrap molasses

Directions:

1. Lightly grease a baking dish (8x8) with cooking spray. Preheat an oven to 375°F.
2. Puree the beans in the blender and pour in a mixing bowl.
3. Ad and mix in the baking powder, salt, applesauce, and molasses.
4. Stir in the flour and cocoa powder; mix well.
5. Add the batter in prepared dish; bake until cooked through for about 35 minutes.

Nutritional Values (Per Serving):

Calories – 143

Fat – 1g

Saturated Fats – 0g

Trans Fats - 0g

Carbohydrates – 32g

Fiber – 3g

Sodium – 263mg

Protein – 3g

Pumpkin Cake Muffins

Prep Time: 8-10 min.

Cooking Time: 20-22 min.

Number of Servings: 24

Freestyle Points per Serving: 2

Ingredients:

- 2 cups pumpkin puree
- 1 cup water
- 1 box yellow cake mix, sugar-free

Directions:

1. Take 24 muffin tins and line them with liner. Preheat an oven to 350°F.
2. Take a mixing bowl (either medium or large size), add and mix all the ingredients in the bowl to mix well with each other.
3. Add into the muffin tins; bake for 22 minutes or until tops are lightly browned.

Nutritional Values (Per Serving):

Calories – 89

Fat – 2g

Saturated Fats – 1g

Trans Fats - 0g

Carbohydrates – 17g

Fiber – 1g

Sodium – 126mg

Protein – 2g

Made in the USA
San Bernardino, CA
04 January 2020

62655920R00069